MARC BROWN

ARTHUR, CLEAN YOUR ROOM!

Step into Reading® Sticker Books

Random House 🏠 New York

Copyright © 1999 by Marc Brown. All rights reserved under International and Pan-American Copyright Conventions. Published in the United States by Random House, Inc., New York, and simultaneously in Canada by Random House of Canada Limited, Toronto.

www.randomhouse.com/kids

Library of Congress Cataloging-in-Publication Data
Brown, Marc Tolon. Arthur, clean your room! / [text and illustrations by] Marc Brown. p. cm.
SUMMARY: His sister D.W. convinces Arthur to have a garage sale after his mother tells him to get rid of the junk in his room, but things do not work out exactly as he had planned.
ISBN 0-679-88467-X (trade) — ISBN 0-679-98467-4 (lib. bdg.)
[1. Aardvark—Fiction. 2. Orderliness—Fiction. 3. Garage sales—Fiction.
4. Brothers and sisters—Fiction.] I. Title. PZ7.B81618Ald 1999 [E]—dc21 98-43341
Printed in the United States of America 10 9 8 7 6 5 4 3 2 1

STEP INTO READING is a registered trademark of Random House, Inc.

ARTHUR® is a registered trademark of Marc Brown.

"Mom, I can't find my Bionic  said Arthur.

"No wonder," Arthur's mother said.

"Look at all this junk!"

"It's not junk," said Arthur.

"It IS junk," she said,

"and I want you to get rid of it—
    NOW!"

"But how can I get rid of it?"
asked Arthur.
"Sell it," said D.W.
"You can make big "

"Have a  sale," said Mother.

"And have it today."

5

D.W. helped Arthur carry of junk outside.
I've always liked
your Jolly Jingle Maker,"
said D.W. "Can I have it?"
"I'm selling it," said Arthur.

GARAGE SALE TODAY

ROCKS

Buster was the first  there.
"I can't believe you're selling
this Bionic Bu[nny] [fi]ghter,"
said Buster. "I don't have a
but I'll trade you my
Bionic   Spy   ."

"Your Bionic Bunny Spy "
said Arthur. "Okay, great trade!"
Buster ran to his
to get them.

Then Francine came along with
a  filled with comic
"My mom is making me get rid
of these," she said sadly.

"Oh, boy, Cool Cat comics!"
said Arthur.

"Wow!" said Francine.

"Is that a real
World Cup Soccer Game?"

"Almost new," said Arthur.

"I'll trade it for your comics."

"All right!" said Francine.

11

News spread, and Arthur's friends

all came with things to trade.

"Binky, that is so cool,"

said Arthur. "What is it?"

"My punching ," said Binky.

"I want to trade it

for your  Sam

"Good de..." said Arthur.

My Own Arthur Story

by ....

Can you write and illustrate a story about Arthur's new garden? Here are some stickers to get you started. Have fun!

Muffy showed up next.
"You've always liked
my clubhouse"
she said. "Want to trade?"
"Sure," said Arthur.
"Is this cute
really yours, Arthur?"
she giggled.
"It's yours now," he said.
"It's never been worn."

The Brain came with a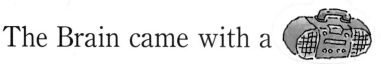

"It needs a little work," he said.

"I'll trade you my

said Sue Ellen.

Prunella traded
he   poster.

Fern had a typewriter
that Arthur really liked.

Arthur was happy.

His old stuff was gone.

D.W. ran to the

"You didn't sell your

Jolly Jingle Maker," she said.

"But I got rid of all my other

old stuff," said Arthur.

"I'll count your money,"

said D.W.

"Well," he said,

"I didn't really get   .."

"But I got all this great new stuff,"
said Arthur.

"If Mom sees this," said D.W.,

"you are in big trouble."

"You're right," he said,

"but what am I going to do?"

"I have a plan,"

whispered D.W.

Later that day, Arthur's mother
went to check his room.
Arthur followed her up the
He crossed his fingers
and held his breath.

"Good job, Arthur," she said.

"You got rid of all your junk."

Just then they heard a big

CRASH!

They ran to D.W.'s room.

Junk was everywhere.

"Dora Winifred!" shouted Mother.

"What is this mess?"

"It's not a mess," said D.W.

"It's business.

Arthur is paying me rent.

And he owes me a

"I don't have a  said Arthur,
"but how about a trade?"